DANGEROUS-DOG HEARINGS AND PROCEDURES

A Guide for Local Governments

🏛 UNC | SCHOOL OF GOVERNMENT

The School of Government at the University of North Carolina at Chapel Hill works to improve the lives of North Carolinians by engaging in practical scholarship that helps public officials and citizens understand and improve state and local government. Established in 1931 as the Institute of Government, the School provides educational, advisory, and research services for state and local governments. The School of Government is also home to a nationally ranked Master of Public Administration program, the North Carolina Judicial College, and specialized centers focused on community and economic development, information technology, and environmental finance.

As the largest university-based local government training, advisory, and research organization in the United States, the School of Government offers up to 200 courses, webinars, and specialized conferences for more than 12,000 public officials each year. In addition, faculty members annually publish approximately 50 books, manuals, reports, articles, bulletins, and other print and online content related to state and local government. The School also produces the *Daily Bulletin Online* each day the General Assembly is in session, reporting on activities for members of the legislature and others who need to follow the course of legislation.

Operating support for the School of Government's programs and activities comes from many sources, including state appropriations, local government membership dues, private contributions, publication sales, course fees, and service contracts.

Visit sog.unc.edu or call 919.966.5381 for more information on the School's courses, publications, programs, and services.

Aimee N. Wall, Dean
Jeffrey B. Welty, Senior Associate Dean for Faculty Affairs
Anita R. Brown-Graham, Associate Dean for Strategic Initiatives
Willow S. Jacobson, Associate Dean for Graduate Studies
Kara A. Millonzi, Associate Dean for Research and Innovation
Lauren G. Partin, Senior Associate Dean For Administration
Sonja Matanovic, Associate Dean for Strategic Communications
Matt Marvin, Associate Dean For Advancement and Partnerships

FACULTY

Whitney Afonso	Jacquelyn Greene	C. Tyler Mulligan
Gregory S. Allison	Timothy Heinle	Kimberly L. Nelson
Rebecca Badgett	Cheryl Daniels Howell	Kristi A. Nickodem
Maureen Berner	Joseph L. Hyde	Obed Pasha
Kirk Boone	James L. Joyce	William C. Rivenbark
Mark F. Botts	Robert P. Joyce	John Rubin
Brittany LaDawn Bromell	Diane M. Juffras	Meredith Smith
Melanie Y. Crenshaw	Joseph Laizure	Daniel Spiegel
Crista M. Cuccaro	Kirsten Leloudis	Carl W. Stenberg III
Leisha DeHart-Davis	Adam Lovelady	John B. Stephens
Shea Riggsbee Denning	James M. Markham	Elliot Stoller
Sara DePasquale	Christopher B. McLaughlin	Charles Szypszak
Kimalee Cottrell Dickerson	Jill D. Moore	Shannon H. Tufts
Phil Dixon, Jr.	Jonathan Q. Morgan	Amy Wade
Belal Elrahal	Taylor Morris	Teshanee T. Williams
Rebecca L. Fisher-Gabbard	Ricardo S. Morse	Kristina M. Wilson

© 2025
School of Government
The University of North Carolina at Chapel Hill

Printed in the United States of America
29 28 27 26 25   1 2 3 4 5
ISBN 978-1-64238-121-4

Contents

Dangerous-Dog Hearings and Procedures

Local governments in North Carolina are required by state law to designate a person or a board to be responsible for determining when a dog in the community is what the law defines as a *potentially dangerous dog*. Local governments also must designate a separate board to hear a dog owner's appeal from the determination that a dog is a potentially dangerous dog.

Beyond that mandate, state law says little about who should be selected for these roles or the procedures that should be followed. Consequently, local governments have significant flexibility to craft schemes for dangerous-dog determinations that are tailored to local conditions, but they do not have the benefit of clear statutory guidance about how these proceedings should work in practice.

This publication is a guide for North Carolina local governments on the law and procedures pertaining to dangerous-dog determinations under state law. While the discussion is supported with footnotes referencing statutes, caselaw, and technical details, the publication is intended for a broad audience of local government officials and employees. It is designed so that a reader may gain a good understanding of the law simply by reading the main text without careful study of the footnotes.[1]

Dangerous Dogs and Potentially Dangerous Dogs Under State Law

Local officials developing or administering a determination scheme in their jurisdiction should understand the generally applicable statewide law concerning dangerous and potentially dangerous dogs. This section first provides an overview of the state law and then discusses the authority for local governments to deviate from state law by adopting ordinances.

---

1. For detailed discussion of North Carolina animal services law, including elements of dangerous-dog law not discussed in this publication, see AIMEE WALL & CHRISTOPHER TYNER, NORTH CAROLINA GUIDE TO ANIMAL SERVICES LAW (UNC School of Government, 2018).

Definitions

North Carolina state law functions primarily by defining both *dangerous* and *potentially dangerous* as applied to dogs, requiring local governments to determine when a dog is potentially dangerous, and providing certain restrictions on the owners of dangerous and potentially dangerous dogs.[2]

The state's definition of *dangerous dog* overlaps with its definition of *potentially dangerous dog*. This overlap can be confusing at first blush, but, as discussed in more detail below, it simply means that a potentially dangerous dog is a type of dangerous dog under state law.

Because a potentially dangerous dog is a type of dangerous dog under the law, this publication usually refers to the *dangerous-dog law* and a *dangerous-dog determination* when discussing North Carolina's statutory scheme concerning dangerous and potentially dangerous dogs. For example, the term *dangerous-dog determination* is used in this publication to refer to the overall process of deciding whether a dog is a potentially dangerous dog under state law and also is used to refer to the decision itself.

North Carolina state law defines a dangerous dog as one that is owned or harbored for the purpose of dogfighting; is trained for dogfighting; has, without provocation, killed or inflicted severe injury on a person; or is determined by a local government to be a potentially dangerous dog.[3]

Dangerous Dog

A *dangerous dog* is one that

- is owned or harbored primarily or in part for the purpose of dogfighting;
- is trained for dogfighting;
- has, without provocation, killed or inflicted severe injury on a person; or
- is determined by a local government to be a *potentially dangerous dog*.

Source: G.S. 67-4.1(a)(1).

Thus, if a local government determines that a dog is potentially dangerous, the dog will be treated as a dangerous dog for the purposes of state law. No determination by a local government is necessary with respect to the other types of dangerous dogs defined by state law. A dog automatically is a dangerous dog under state law if it is owned, harbored, or trained for dogfighting or if it has inflicted a severe injury upon a person without provocation.

---

2. *See generally* Chapter 67, Article 1A of the North Carolina General Statutes [hereinafter G.S.].

3. G.S. 67-4.1(a)(1). A severe injury is "any physical injury that results in broken bones or disfiguring lacerations or requires cosmetic surgery or hospitalization." *Id.* § (a)(5).

State law defines a potentially dangerous dog as one determined by a local government representative or board to have "[i]nflicted a bite on a person that resulted in broken bones or disfiguring lacerations or required cosmetic surgery or hospitalization";[4] "[k]illed or inflicted severe injury upon a domestic animal when not on the owner's real property"; or "[a]pproached a person when not on the owner's property in a vicious or terrorizing manner in an apparent attitude of attack."[5]

Potentially Dangerous Dog

A *potentially dangerous dog* is one that has been determined by a local government to have

- inflicted a bite on a person that resulted in broken bones or disfiguring lacerations or required cosmetic surgery or hospitalization;
- killed or inflicted severe injury upon a domestic animal when not on the owner's real property; or
- approached a person when not on the owner's property in a vicious or terrorizing manner in an apparent attitude of attack.

Source: G.S. 67-4.1(a)(2).

The dangerous-dog law does not apply to a dog being used by a law enforcement officer to carry out the officer's official duties or to a dog being used in a lawful hunt.[6] It does not apply in situations where a hunting, herding, or predator-control dog, working as such under its owner or keeper's control or on its owner or keeper's property, injures a domestic animal that is appropriate to the dog's work.[7] It also does not apply in situations where the dog injures a person as that person is committing a crime or a willful trespass or other tort; is attempting to commit a crime; or is tormenting, abusing, or assaulting the dog. Finally, the dangerous-dog law does not apply if the injury is to a person who has tormented, abused, or assaulted the dog in the past.[8]

---

4. The types of injuries specified under the statute are the same as those constituting severe injury under the statutory definition discussed above, in note 3.

5. G.S. 67-4.1(a)(2).

6. *Id.* § (b).

7. *Id.* The law does not specify what proof is sufficient to establish that a dog was working as a "hunting dog," "herding dog," or "predator control dog," nor does the law define those terms.

8. *Id.*

Exceptions

The dangerous-dog law does not apply in the following circumstances:

- The dog was being used by a law enforcement officer to carry out the officer's official duties.
- The dog was being used in a lawful hunt.
- The injury or damage was to a domestic animal appropriate to the dog's work while it was working as a hunting, herding, or predator-control dog under its owner or keeper's control or on its owner or keeper's property.
- The injury was sustained by a person who was committing a crime; committing a willful trespass or other tort; attempting to commit a crime; or tormenting, abusing, or assaulting the dog.
- The injury was sustained by a person who had tormented, abused, or assaulted the dog in the past.

Source: G.S. 67-4.1(b).

Dangerous-Dog Determinations and Appellate Boards

Local governments must designate a person or a board responsible for making initial determinations of whether a dog in the community is a potentially dangerous dog as defined by state law.[9] The need to make this determination usually arises when local officials in animal services or public safety respond to or receive a report of a bite, an attack, or some other incident involving someone's dog. The law does not specify a time period within which an initial dangerous-dog determination must then be made. The law also does not identify any specific person or board to be charged with the responsibility for making the initial determination.

In some jurisdictions, an individual local government employee, such as an animal services official or the local health director,[10] may make the initial determination; in others, a board established specifically for this purpose does so. As another alternative, the responsibility could be assigned to a board that has a primary purpose other than making dangerous-dog determinations. Readers unfamiliar with the dangerous-dog law may find the sample form for initial determinations provided in Appendix A helpful for gaining a more concrete understanding of what an initial determination may look like in practice.

---

9. *Id.* § (c). The statute assigns this designation responsibility to "[t]he county or municipal authority responsible for animal control." *Id.* This publication uses the more general term *local government.*

10. Note that apart from the dangerous-dog law, G.S. 130A-200 grants local health directors the authority to declare an animal to be "vicious and a menace to the public health when the animal has attacked a person causing bodily harm without being teased, molested, provoked, beaten, tortured or otherwise harmed." Such an animal must be confined to its owner's property unless it is leashed and accompanied by a responsible adult.

In addition to designating a person or board to make the initial determination of whether a dog is potentially dangerous, state law requires that local governments designate a separate board to hear appeals from the initial determination.[11] A dog owner may appeal to the appellate board by filing written objections with the board within three days of the initial determination.[12] A sample form for written objections is provided in Appendix B. The board must schedule a hearing within ten days of the filing of objections.[13]

Local governments should devise a method of providing an owner with written notice of the scheduling of the hearing, as well as general information about the nature of the hearing. A sample notice is provided in Appendix C. Readers unfamiliar with the dangerous-dog law may find the sample opening statement for hearings provided in Appendix D useful for gaining a clearer understanding of how appellate-board proceedings may be conducted.

As with initial determinations, local governments have discretion to take a variety of approaches to appellate boards. A board may be established specifically to hear appeals from dangerous-dog determinations, or the responsibility may be given to a board that has another primary purpose. If a board is established specifically to hear appeals, it is advisable that one member be selected to chair the board and preside over hearings by, for example, delivering opening remarks, regulating the presentation of evidence, announcing the board's decision, and generally controlling the proceedings. Appellate boards should consist of an odd number of members so that it is not possible for the board to reach a voting deadlock and be unable to render a decision at an appeal hearing.

An owner who wishes to appeal an appellate board's decision may do so by filing a notice of appeal and a petition for review in the superior court of the county in which the appellate board is located. The owner's notice of appeal must be filed within ten days of the board's final decision.[14]

Figure 1. Dangerous-Dog Proceedings

Initial Determination		Appellate-Board Hearing		Superior Court De Novo Appeal
A designated person or board makes an initial determination whether a dog is a "potentially dangerous dog"	Dog owner **objects**	A designated board conducts a hearing on the dog owner's objection to the initial determination	Dog owner **appeals**	Superior court judge conducts an entirely new hearing

---

11. G.S. 67-4.1(c). As with the initial determination, the statute assigns this designation responsibility to "[t]he county or municipal authority responsible for animal control." *Id.* This publication uses the more general term *local government.*

12. *Id.*

13. *Id.* The statute does not specify whether it is the act of scheduling the hearing that must occur within ten days or whether the hearing itself must occur within ten days.

14. *Id.*

Within this general framework, the local government has significant flexibility to adopt an approach to initial determinations and appellate review that is suitable for its community.

Restrictions on Owners

Under state law, an owner of a dangerous or potentially dangerous dog[15] faces several criminally enforceable restrictions on the owner's manner of care for the dog as well as criminal liability for certain attacks by the dog. *Owner* is defined as "any person or legal entity that has a possessory property right in a dog."[16] The restrictions upon owners are set out in G.S. 67-4.2, and violating them is a Class 3 misdemeanor. A dangerous dog must not be left unattended on its owner's property "unless [it] is confined indoors, in a securely closed and locked pen, or in another structure designed to restrain the dog." A dangerous dog must not be allowed off the owner's property unless it is leashed (or otherwise securely restrained) and muzzled. If an owner transfers ownership or possession of a dangerous dog, that owner must give two written notices: One notice must go to the local government that made the dangerous-dog determination, providing the new owner or possessor's name and address, and one to the new owner or possessor, specifying the dog's dangerous behavior and the local government's determination that the dog is potentially dangerous.

Dangerous-Dog Restrictions

- The dog must not be left unattended on the owner's property "unless the dog is confined indoors, in a securely enclosed and locked pen, or in another structure designed to restrain the dog."
- The dog must not be allowed off the owner's property unless it is leashed (or otherwise securely restrained) and muzzled.
- If the owner transfers ownership or possession of the dog, the owner must provide written notice to the local government that made the determination that the dog is a potentially dangerous dog. The notice must state the name and address of the dog's new owner or possessor.
- If the owner transfers ownership or possession of the dog, the owner must provide written notice to the new owner or possessor, specifying the dog's dangerous behavior and the local government's determination that the dog is potentially dangerous.

Source: G.S. 67-4.2.

---

15. The same restrictions and penalties apply to dogs that meet the statutory definition of a dangerous dog but that have not been formally declared by the local government to be potentially dangerous.

16. G.S. 67-4.1(a)(3).

If a dangerous dog attacks someone and causes physical injuries that require medical care costing more than one hundred dollars, its owner may be charged with a Class 1 misdemeanor.[17] Additionally, the owner of a dangerous dog is strictly liable in civil damages for any injuries or property damage the dog inflicts upon a person, a person's property, or another animal.[18]

Local Ordinances

Cities and counties have broad power to regulate animals by ordinance, and many local governments have used this power to adopt dangerous-dog ordinances over the years. A number of local governments have ordinances that were already in place when the state's statutory framework for dangerous dogs was enacted in 1989, and some ordinances have been adopted or amended since.

The general rule in North Carolina is that local ordinances may only supplement or complement state law; they must not replace it or conflict with it.[19] However, this general rule does not apply in the context of dangerous-dog ordinances because of a statute specifically stating that the state dangerous-dog law must not be "construed to prevent a city or county from adopting or enforcing its own program for control of dangerous dogs."[20] Local governments, therefore, have leeway to craft dangerous-dog programs that differ from state law to a greater extent than typically is the case when ordinance-making authority is used to address an issue that already is the subject of state law.

Jurisdictions across the state take varied approaches to dangerous-dog ordinances. Some have not adopted any ordinances, and thus rely entirely on the framework provided by state law. A few jurisdictions have adopted ordinances that simply restate the state dangerous-dog law, though this approach is not recommended as local ordinances typically should not duplicate state law.[21] Some have adopted ordinances that cross-reference the state law and supplement it with procedural details, such as the composition of the appeals boards, or include more specificity related to restrictions imposed by state law, such as detailed information about the type or construction of enclosures required for the dogs. Other jurisdictions have adopted wholly comprehensive schemes for addressing dangerous dogs.

This publication is written with the assumption that a jurisdiction is operating largely under the dangerous-dog scheme provided by state law. As a result,

---

17. *Id.* § 4.3.

18. *Id.* § 4.4.

19. G.S. 160A-174(b). While these limitations are named only in the state statute governing municipalities, the courts have consistently extended their application to counties. *See* State v. Tenore, 280 N.C. 238, 248 (1972).

20. G.S. 67-4.5.

21. In other contexts, state law explicitly prohibits enacting ordinances that are identical to state law. *See* G.S. 160A-174(b)(6); *Tenore*, 280 N.C. 238. Beyond this, a jurisdiction that intends for state law to control dangerous-dog issues arguably should refrain from restating that law, as doing so raises the possibility that the local ordinance and state law will fall out of harmony if state law is revised.

significant portions of the discussion may bear little resemblance to the actual practice in a jurisdiction that has chosen to depart significantly from state law by enacting a comprehensive dangerous-dog scheme by local ordinance.

Due Process of Law in Local Government Decisions

As a matter of both good governance and constitutional law, local governments must act fairly when making decisions that affect citizens' rights. Because dangerous-dog proceedings may result in limitation of a dog owner's rights,[22] the proceedings must be structured in a way that ensures protection of the dog owner's constitutional right to due process of law.[23]

North Carolina courts have recognized that due process is a fluid and flexible concept and that the level of procedural due process required in governmental decisions depends upon the balance between individual and governmental interests in the decision at issue.[24] The courts have not specified exactly what procedures are sufficient for dangerous-dog determinations. Nevertheless, at least some standards typically associated with trials or other government tribunals ought to be applied during these proceedings to ensure that citizens are afforded fundamental fairness in determinations of whether a dog is potentially dangerous. Fair proceedings protect the rights of citizens, engender community confidence in local government decision-making, and shield against allegations that a local government has acted unlawfully.

The following sections discuss two central components of due process of law—an unbiased, impartial decision-maker and an opportunity for a hearing—and their applicability to the dangerous-dog-determination process.

An Unbiased, Impartial Decision-Maker

A minimum requirement of fair proceedings is that decision-makers must be neutral third parties who are unbiased and impartial.[25] This notion is implicit in the statutory requirement that the appellate board be "separate" from the decision-maker who makes the initial determination that a dog is potentially

---

22. At minimum, a determination that a dog is potentially dangerous has the effect of limiting the owner's property rights with respect to the dog because the owner becomes obligated to confine and secure the dog and to abide by certain requirements related to the transfer of ownership or possession of the dog.

23. A person's right to due process is protected under both the state and federal constitutions. *See* Crump v. Bd. of Educ., 326 N.C. 603, 607 (1990); *In re* Lamm, 116 N.C. App. 382, 384 (1994), *aff'd per curiam*, 341 N.C. 196 (1995).

24. *Crump*, 326 N.C. at 615; *Lamm*, 116 N.C. App. at 385.

25. *Crump*, 326 N.C. at 615 ("An unbiased, impartial decision-maker is essential to due process.").

dangerous,[26] a requirement which means that those who make the initial determination must not also sit on the appellate board that reviews those decisions.

Being unbiased and impartial means that a person is capable of making a decision with an open mind while fairly taking account of the totality of the circumstances of a given situation.[27] Being unbiased and impartial ensures integrity in a decision-maker's role in dangerous-dog determinations.

Two common things that would keep someone from being an unbiased and impartial decision-maker are having a preexisting opinion of a dog's dangerousness that is not susceptible to change or having a conflict of interest.[28] Someone might have a conflict of interest in a dangerous-dog determination by having either a personal interest in the outcome or a close relationship with someone who would be affected by the outcome.

It is advisable to develop a plan for situations where a decision-maker must be recused from a particular dangerous-dog determination because of an unchangeable preexisting opinion or a conflict of interest. Examples of such a plan for a board include specifying that a decision will be reached by majority vote of the remaining, nonrecused members or specifying that any recused member will be replaced by an alternate member. An example of such a plan for a single decision-maker charged with initial dangerous-dog determinations would be specifying an alternate person to make the initial determination in cases where recusal is necessary.

Other than the mandate that an initial dangerous-dog decision not be reviewed on appeal by a person who made the decision, the state dangerous-dog law leaves discretion to local governments to decide who should serve as a decision-maker in dangerous-dog determinations.[29]

---

26. G.S. 67-4.1(c).

27. *Crump*, 326 N.C. at 620 (stating that a fundamental notion of due process is that decision-makers have an open mind and fairly evaluate evidence that is presented). *See generally* David W. Owens & Adam S. Lovelady, Quasi-Judicial Handbook, ch. 3 (UNC School of Government, 2024) (discussing impartiality) [hereinafter Quasi-Judicial Handbook].

28. Quasi-Judicial Handbook, ch. 3 (describing analogous law in the context of decisions of local planning and development boards).

29. Note that there are statutory and constitutional disqualifications from office that in some circumstances potentially could prevent a person from serving as a decision-maker in dangerous-dog determinations. The state constitution prohibits felons from holding office until their rights of citizenship are restored, and both the state constitution and state statute prohibit a person from holding more than two elected or appointed offices. *See* Quasi-Judicial Handbook, ch. 2 (explaining the limitation on dual office-holding in more detail). No North Carolina appellate case has directly considered these limitations in the context of dangerous-dog determinations.

Common Questions About Bias and Impartiality

May a person who directly investigates an incident decide whether a dog is potentially dangerous on the basis of that incident?

Some jurisdictions rely on animal services officials or law enforcement officers to make initial or subsequent determinations of whether a dog is potentially dangerous. Because these individuals also may have responsibility for responding to and investigating the incident that is the basis for a dog being declared potentially dangerous, the question may arise whether they qualify as unbiased and impartial decision-makers.

Direct involvement in the investigation of an incident giving rise to a dangerous-dog proceeding probably is insufficient standing alone to disqualify a person from being a decision-maker in the proceeding. In fact, there likely is some efficiency in designating an animal services official or law enforcement officer as the party responsible for deciding whether a dog is potentially dangerous because that person likely will be well positioned to assess the facts of the incident and the credibility of the parties involved.

What if a decision-maker knows the dog owner or other party to the incident?

A mere association between a decision-maker and a party is insufficient standing alone to disqualify the decision-maker from a dangerous-dog proceeding. However, a decision-maker's ability to be unbiased and impartial may be called into question if the decision-maker has a close personal relationship with one of the parties involved. A good test for whether recusal is necessary is asking whether a reasonable third party would have grounds to question the decision-maker's impartiality because of the closeness or nature of the relationship.

What if a decision-maker in a dangerous-dog proceeding has prior knowledge of the incident at issue or other incidents involving the same dog?

As a general matter, decisions in dangerous-dog hearings should be based on evidence that is presented at the hearing because it is more likely that such evidence will be tested for reliability, as discussed in more detail later in this publication. However, the ability to be unbiased and impartial is not necessarily diminished merely because the decision-maker comes to a proceeding with prior knowledge of the incident at issue or of other incidents involving the dog. So long as the decision-maker approaches the proceeding with an open mind and fairly weighs the evidence, prior knowledge does not necessitate recusal.

Common Questions About Bias and Impartiality (continued)

What if a decision-maker has ex parte communications about the incident at issue?

An ex parte communication occurs when a decision-maker communicates about the case in the absence of a party or other decision-makers. For example, if a member of a board responsible for dangerous-dog hearings has a private conversation with a person who witnessed an incident giving rise to a pending dangerous-dog determination, that conversation would be an ex parte communication because it occurred in the absence of other board members and any other parties to the incident. As a general rule, decision-makers should avoid ex parte communications in order to preserve the fairness of the proceedings and public confidence in them. Ex parte communications are not necessarily disqualifying, but any such communication should be disclosed to all parties and other board members during the proceeding.

What if a decision-maker believes that they have a conflict of interest affecting their ability to be unbiased and impartial?

In that situation, the decision-maker should recuse. As discussed in more detail elsewhere in this publication, it is important for local governments to structure dangerous-dog determinations such that the process remains functional even when recusal is required. This may be done in various ways, including by designating an alternate decision-maker for initial determinations and describing how boards will make decisions when a member must be recused.

What if a party to the proceeding asserts that a decision-maker has a conflict of interest?

It is possible that a dog owner or other party to a proceeding may assert that a decision-maker has a conflict of interest. A decision-maker should be recused if such an assertion is supported by sufficient reliable evidence to cause a reasonable third party to question the decision-maker's ability to be unbiased and impartial.

An Opportunity for a Hearing

A recurring due-process question in situations where a local government makes a decision that limits a person's rights[30] is whether the person is entitled to a hearing prior to the decision being rendered. When a hearing is not required, a local government is said to be able to act in a *summary* manner. If a hearing is required, the

---

30. As noted above, at minimum, a determination that a dog is potentially dangerous limits the owner's property rights with respect to the dog.

next questions are what level of formality in the hearing is necessary and to what degree and in what manner the person is entitled to participate.

The state dangerous-dog law specifies that a proceeding before a dangerous-dog appellate board is a hearing,[31] but it does not specify whether a hearing is required in connection with an initial determination, and no North Carolina appellate case has decided the issue. As discussed below, initial determinations likely may be made without a hearing.

Initial Dangerous-Dog Determinations

As mentioned above, due process is a flexible concept and the procedures necessary to ensure fairness depend on the balance between the individual and governmental interests at issue.[32] The courts have held that in some situations, it is permissible to make an initial decision limiting a person's rights without holding a hearing, so long as there is an opportunity for the person to receive a prompt and meaningful hearing afterward.[33] Under this reasoning, courts have upheld, among other things, the constitutionality of summary proceedings terminating social-security disability benefits,[34] suspending driver's licenses for impaired driving,[35] and suspending an attorney's license to practice law.[36]

Since state law provides dog owners with an opportunity to object to an initial determination and receive a relatively prompt hearing before an appellate board,[37] it is likely that the initial determination may be made summarily and without a hearing.[38]

To ensure that initial dangerous-dog determinations made in a summary manner are reasonably reliable, it is advisable that a local government set out a procedure for the decision-maker to follow and document when making an initial determination.[39] This procedure need not be extensive, but it should require the decision-maker to find that there is a reasonably reliable factual basis to support a determination that a dog is a potentially dangerous dog under state law.

---

31. G.S. 67-4.1(c).

32. *In re* Lamm, 116 N.C. App. 382, 385 (1994), *aff'd per curiam*, 341 N.C. 196 (1995).

33. *Id.* at 386.

34. Mathews v. Eldridge, 424 U.S. 319 (1976).

35. Henry v. Edmisten, 315 N.C. 474 (1986).

36. *Lamm*, 116 N.C. App. 382.

37. Recall as well that an appellate board's decision may be further appealed to the superior court.

38. It also is arguable that the fact that G.S. 67-4.1(c) specifically requires a "hearing" for appeals but simply a "determination" initially is evidence that, at least as a statutory matter, a hearing is not required at this stage.

39. *Henry*, 315 N.C. at 484 (explaining that when a local government acts summarily it still must follow procedures that are "designed to provide a reasonably reliable basis" for its decision).

Initial Dangerous-Dog Determinations Without a Hearing

Local governments should establish procedures for ensuring that initial dangerous-dog determinations made in a summary manner without a hearing are reasonably reliable.

As state law requires that a dog owner be notified in writing of an initial determination that the dog in question is a potentially dangerous dog, along with documentation of the reasons for the decision, it may be desirable to integrate the decision-making procedure into the required written notice as a unified document that also apprises the dog owner of the option to object to the initial determination and receive a hearing before an appellate board. A sample form for such a document is provided in Appendix A.

Appellate-Board Hearings

The remainder of this publication focuses on procedures for dangerous-dog hearings and provides practical suggestions related to them. Because state law specifically requires that the appellate board conduct a hearing if a dog owner objects to an initial determination, the discussion that follows mostly refers to appellate-board hearings. However, the same or similar principles could be applied if a local government decides to offer a hearing before the person or board responsible for making the initial determination.[40]

Overview

Dangerous-dog hearings should be conducted in compliance with North Carolina law governing open meetings and public records.[41] This generally means that the hearings should take place in sessions open to the public, that full and accurate minutes of the sessions should be created and maintained, and that any record made or received in connection with a hearing is a public record.[42]

Dangerous-dog hearings should include, at least to some degree, the fundamental elements of fair hearings that courts recognize as sufficient to protect the

---

40. As discussed above, it is likely that a hearing is not required before an initial determination, but a local government has discretion to structure its own dangerous-dog scheme.

41. *See generally* G.S. ch. 143, art. 33C.

42. For more detailed information about open meetings and public records, see Quasi-Judicial Handbook, ch. 3; Frayda S. Bluestein & David M. Lawrence, Open Meetings and Local Governments in North Carolina (UNC School of Government, 8th ed. 2017); David M. Lawrence, Public Records Law for North Carolina Local Governments (UNC School of Government, 2d ed. 2010).

right to due process.[43] Generally speaking, the elements of a fair hearing before an unbiased and impartial decision-maker include the parties' right to offer evidence; the requirement that any testimony be sworn as truthful; an opportunity to cross-examine adverse witnesses and inspect nontestimonial exhibits; and the requirement that findings of fact be written and supported by competent, substantial, and material evidence.[44]

Elements of Fair Hearings

- The parties' right to offer evidence
- The requirement that any testimony be sworn as truthful
- An opportunity to cross-examine adverse witnesses and inspect nontestimonial exhibits
- The requirement that findings of fact be written and supported by competent, substantial, and material evidence

---

It is not clear that each of the elements listed above is required in dangerous-dog hearings,[45] particularly in light of the fact that state law allows for a further appeal

---

43. When characterizing local government proceedings that affect an individual's legal rights, North Carolina courts sometimes differentiate between *administrative* and *quasi-judicial* proceedings. *See, e.g.*, Crump v. Bd. of Educ., 326 N.C. 603, 622 (1990) ("[W]hether termed administrative or quasi-judicial, the [local board of education's] action in this case, involving resolution of disputed facts and selection among alternate sanctions, was required to afford [the petitioner], at a minimum, an unbiased hearing in accord with principles of due process."); Maines v. City of Greensboro, 300 N.C. 126, 133 (1980) (characterizing a departmental hearing on whether a city employee had become ineligible to work as a fireman because he no longer resided within the city limits as required by local ordinance as an "administrative determination"). A person typically is entitled to a greater level of procedural due process in quasi-judicial proceedings because decision-makers exercise more discretion in these proceedings compared with proceedings that are merely administrative. While the courts have not specifically decided whether dangerous-dog hearings are quasi-judicial or administrative in nature, they have some hallmarks of quasi-judicial proceedings. *See In re* Mitchell, 88 N.C. App. 602, 605 (1988) (stating that while the distinction between a quasi-judicial determination and an administrative decision is "not precisely defined," courts tend to consider proceedings to be quasi-judicial when they involve notice, a hearing, and an opportunity to appeal an unfavorable outcome).

44. These elements are recognized by courts as components of fair hearings. *See, e.g.*, Wolff v. McDonnell, 418 U.S. 539, 556–73 (1974) (prison disciplinary proceedings for deprivation of "good-time credits"); Goldberg v. Kelly, 397 U.S. 254, 268–69 (1970) (proceedings for welfare termination).

45. *See* Peace v. Emp. Sec. Comm'n, 349 N.C. 315, 324 (1998) (noting that evidentiary hearings are not universally required before the government may infringe on individual property rights).

heard de novo before a superior court judge.[46] However, a proceeding that offers all the elements is certain to guarantee due process.

Local governments have discretion to decide which elements to incorporate into their hearings and how to do so. Some local governments may choose to hold relatively formal hearings involving robust implementation of each of the listed procedural elements, while others may choose to hold relatively informal hearings involving minimal evidentiary presentation.

Discretion on Hearing Formality

Local governments may choose whether to offer relatively formal dangerous-dog hearings that involve robust presentation of evidence and cross-examination or relatively informal hearings with minimal presentation of evidence.

The sections that follow discuss how the elements of fair hearings may be integrated into dangerous-dog hearings. It is important to bear in mind that many dog owners will probably be unfamiliar with how these proceedings work. Therefore, an appellate board may wish to begin its hearings with an opening statement that explains the nature of the proceeding.[47]

Orienting all participants around a common understanding of the proceedings through an opening statement makes hearings more orderly and efficient. Additionally, a well-crafted opening statement can help ensure that hearings are conducted with sufficient due-process protections. Such a statement can be used to set out the initial determination that is the basis for the appeal; describe the role of all participants; provide an opportunity for the board to disclose conflicts of interest, bias, or ex parte communications; explain how the board will hear evidence; describe how the board will determine what evidence is admissible; state the standard by which the board will render its decision; and explain that the dog owner has the right to appeal an unfavorable determination to the superior court. A sample opening statement is provided in Appendix D.

The Right to Offer Evidence and Otherwise Participate in a Hearing

Presentation of evidence to the appellate board, and particularly a dog owner's opportunity to do so in some manner, is the central element of a dangerous-dog hearing. Evidence introduced at the hearing builds the record that serves as the

---

46. See page 25 for this part of the process. When the superior court hears an appeal *de novo* (anew), that means that the hearing is conducted without regard to any previous proceedings, as though they had not occurred.

47. *See* Quasi-Judicial Handbook, ch. 4 (suggesting that land use boards give an opening statement because "[c]larifying the nature of [an] evidentiary hearing sets the stage for proper procedures").

basis for the appellate board's ultimate determination of whether a dog is a potentially dangerous dog.

A general rule of hearings and other legal proceedings is that a person must have a specific and substantial interest in the proceeding to be entitled to participate in it as a party by offering evidence, examining adverse evidence, and otherwise presenting a case. When a person has a sufficient interest in a proceeding to be entitled to participate as a party, the person is said in legal terminology to have *standing*.[48]

State law does not specifically require that a person have standing in a dangerous-dog proceeding to present evidence to the appellate board, but the concept of standing can be helpful for local governments developing procedures for dangerous-dog hearings. Limiting participation in a hearing to persons who have standing helps to focus the hearing on the ultimate issue of a dog's dangerousness and plays a part in ensuring that evidence that is presented is relevant and reliable. In most cases, only the dog owner will have an interest in the hearing that is sufficient for participation as a party.

Standing: The Right to Actively Participate in a Hearing

A person must have a specific and substantial interest in a dangerous-dog proceeding to be entitled to offer evidence, examine adverse evidence, and otherwise present a case. Usually, only the dog owner will have the right to actively participate in the hearing in this way.

A dog owner may wish to be represented at a hearing by an attorney. A local government is free to allow such representation but likely is not obligated to do so. If a local government allows representation, the dog owner may not be represented by a person who is not an attorney.[49]

Local governments have significant discretion over the manner in which an owner's case may be presented to the appellate board, so long as the opportunity to do so is meaningful. An owner could be permitted to directly call witnesses, participate in cross-examination, and introduce exhibits. Alternatively, an owner could be permitted to provide a list of witnesses, questions, and exhibits for the board to call, pose, and consider. Regardless of the extent of active participation that is permitted, at minimum owners should be given an opportunity to make a statement of their case to the board.

---

48. *See generally Standing*, Black's Law Dictionary (12th ed. 2024).

49. *See* N.C. State Bar, Quasi-Judicial Hearings on Zoning and Land Use, 2006 Authorized Practice Advisory Op. 1 (Oct. 20, 2006) (construing G.S. 84-2.1 and G.S. 84-4 to prohibit nonlawyers from appearing in a representative capacity at a quasi-judicial proceeding).

It is important to note that while usually only an owner will be entitled to actively participate in the hearing as a party, other individuals may participate as witnesses. Witnesses provide testimony, typically in response to questions posed by the board or the owner, but, unlike parties, are not entitled to call or cross-examine other witnesses or to make arguments to the board.

As with the manner in which dog owners are permitted to present their cases to the board, local governments have significant discretion to establish how evidence that a dog is potentially dangerous may be presented. In some jurisdictions, this presentation may be accomplished largely through participation in the hearing by board members, who may call or cross-examine witnesses or introduce other evidence. Under this arrangement, the appellate board operates in a hybrid role of both developing the record and making a final determination, based on that record, of whether a dog is dangerous. Alternatively, some jurisdictions may choose to designate a specific person, such as an animal services official, to offer evidence and otherwise participate in the hearing as the party advocating for a finding that a dog is potentially dangerous.[50] Under this arrangement, the appellate board would operate in a role akin to that of a judge in a more formal legal proceeding.

Evidentiary Guidelines

The nature of evidence that is introduced in a dangerous-dog hearing is likely to vary significantly from case to case, depending on, among other things, the facts at hand and the degree of formality with which a local government has chosen to conduct its hearings.

At one side of the spectrum, a hearing conducted with the minimum formality sufficient to satisfy due-process requirements may involve no more than the appellate board's examination of the factual basis for the initial determination, and a brief opportunity to hear the owner's side of the story and an explanation for the objection.[51] At the other, a relatively formal hearing may involve testimony by witnesses, cross-examination, and the presentation and inspection of various exhibits. The hearing procedures chosen by many local governments likely will fall somewhere between these extremes.

No matter the level of formality, certain evidentiary guidelines are helpful for appellate boards to keep in mind: witnesses should have personal knowledge of the facts to which they will testify, their testimony should be sworn, the evidence

---

50. A local government attorney probably should not be designated as the person responsible for offering evidence at a dangerous-dog hearing if there is the possibility that such an attorney will be responsible for advising the appellate board or local government on legal issues that may arise from the hearing. However, if the attorney is not responsible for advising the board or advising the local government on legal issues that could arise from the hearing, this sort of conflict of interest likely will not occur.

51. *Cf.* Goss v. Lopez, 419 U.S. 565, 577–84 (1975) (approving of analogous procedures as providing sufficient due-process protection in the context of a student being suspended from school).

presented should be relevant to the board's decision, and any nontestimonial exhibits should be authentic.

Evidentiary Guidelines

- Witnesses should have personal knowledge of the facts to which they will testify.
- Witnesses' testimony should be sworn.
- Evidence presented should be relevant to the board's decision.
- Any nontestimonial exhibits should be authentic.

Drawn from the rules of evidence applicable to court proceedings, these guidelines are not mandatory[52] but help to ensure that the record that forms the basis for the appellate board's decision is built on a reliable foundation. These guidelines also help to promote efficient hearings. The sections that follow discuss these guidelines in more detail.

Sworn Testimony of Witnesses with Firsthand Knowledge

Witnesses should have firsthand knowledge of the facts to which they are testifying and should swear to testify truthfully. The requirement of firsthand knowledge of a fact typically means that the witness personally observed or experienced the event or circumstance described in the testimony rather than learning about it from someone else.[53] When a person has this kind of firsthand knowledge, it is said in legal terminology that they are *competent to testify* about the particular matter they have observed.[54]

Firsthand Knowledge

A witness has firsthand knowledge of a fact when the witness personally observed or experienced the event or circumstance described in the testimony rather than learning about it from someone else.

The firsthand-knowledge requirement benefits appellate-board hearings by limiting the pool of potential witnesses to people who are likely to provide testimony that is useful for the board's decision-making. Requiring that witnesses swear to testify truthfully protects the integrity of the proceedings.

---

52. The rules of evidence apply only to actions and proceedings in North Carolina courts. *See* North Carolina Rules of Evidence, G.S. 8C-1, r. 1101(a).
53. *See generally* 1 McCORMICK ON EVIDENCE § 10 (Robert P. Mosteller ed., 9th ed. 2025).
54. *Id.*

It may be the case that a party seeks to present statements from a witness by way of an affidavit or a writing rather than live testimony. Appellate boards have discretion to permit the presentation of this material but generally should subject statements made in affidavits or writings to the same basic requirements as live testimony. Ideally, the affidavit or writing should include an acknowledgment from the witness that the content of the affidavit or writing is truthful and based on firsthand knowledge. In some instances, these elements of reliability may be apparent from the content of the statement, the identity of the witness, or some other characteristic of the writing.

Even when a particular witness is competent to testify or provide a statement at a hearing because of firsthand knowledge, the testimony or statement should be limited to information that is relevant to the appellate board's decision. Relevance is discussed immediately below.

Evidence Relevant to the Appellate Board's Decision

An appellate board should be mindful to ensure that the evidence offered is relevant to the board's ultimate decision of whether a dog is potentially dangerous under state law. Unlike trial judges, who can rely on attorneys in civil and criminal cases to object when the opposing party attempts to introduce irrelevant evidence, the board members themselves are largely responsible for limiting irrelevant testimony or exhibits in dangerous-dog hearings.

Evidence is relevant if it has a logical tendency to prove a fact at issue. This generally means that evidence is relevant to a dangerous-dog hearing if it has a tendency to prove whether a dog has done any of the things that merit designating it a potentially dangerous dog or whether any of the exceptions provided by state law are applicable to the case.

It typically will be necessary for appellate boards to hear some evidence that is ancillary to the main issues listed above.[55] Most witness testimony will require some general narrative that provides context, credibility, and a foundation for the witness's observations. For example, a witness who observed a dog approach another person in a vicious manner in a public park might testify not only to that specific observation but also to the general layout of the park, the weather and lighting conditions, and what the witness was doing in the moments surrounding this observation.

Appellate boards have significant discretion to control the presentation of evidence and are not required to allow the presentation of evidence that, while relevant, lacks probative value.[56] An illustration of evidence that is relevant but lacks substantial probative value is testimony that is needlessly repetitive or cumulative. For example, if a person has suffered a broken bone caused by a dog bite and the injury is well documented with authentic photographs and medical records, a

---

55. *See generally id.* § 185.1.
56. *Id.* § 185.2.

board may decide that it is unnecessary to hear testimony from the professionals who treated the injury.

Relevant Evidence with Probative Value

Evidence is relevant if it has a logical tendency to prove a fact at issue. Some evidence may be relevant but nevertheless lack substantial probative value because it is repetitive, is cumulative, or for some other reason does not assist the appellate board.

Prohibiting irrelevant testimony is desirable for at least two reasons. As a matter of constitutional due process and good governance, the board's ultimate decision should be supported by substantial and material evidence. Evidence that is irrelevant is neither substantial nor material to the board's decision. Limiting irrelevant testimony also is desirable because doing so increases the efficiency of hearings.

Authentic Exhibits

Dangerous-dog hearings may involve the presentation of documents, photographs, videos, electronic communications, or other forms of what is called *nontestimonial evidence*.[57] This wide variety of nontestimonial evidence often is referred to using the general term *exhibit*.

Common exhibits at a dangerous-dog hearing may include an investigator's incident report, the initial dangerous-dog determination, photographs of an injury, medical records, and electronic correspondence such as text messages or emails. No matter the form, it is important to ensure that exhibits offered as evidence are authentic, meaning that the exhibit really is what it is purported to be rather than a fake or a misrepresentation.

Because of the wide variety of exhibits that may be offered at a hearing, the factual variations of different cases, and the range of purposes for which exhibits may be offered, it is difficult to provide comprehensive guidelines about the process of authenticating exhibits.[58] However, for the purposes of dangerous-dog hearings, it is sufficient for a board to require that the party who offers an exhibit provide a credible explanation that the exhibit actually is what the party claims it to be.

---

57. *Id.* § 212.

58. A detailed discussion of authentication is provided in Chapter 22 of *McCormick on Evidence*, cited in the preceding footnotes.

> ## Authentic Exhibits
>
> An appellate board can ensure that exhibits are authentic by requiring the party presenting the exhibit to provide a credible explanation that the exhibit actually is what the party claims it to be.

As an example, if a dog owner wishes to introduce a video that was filmed by a bystander, the dog owner may authenticate the video by identifying who filmed it, explaining how the dog owner obtained it, and assuring the board that it has not been altered or manipulated. Alternatively, the bystander could be called as a witness to provide this information or could provide an affidavit or statement. Some exhibits, such as medical records or business records, may provide some assurance of authenticity on their face, such as official letterhead or other distinctive markings. A chart providing examples of common nontestimonial evidence and potential methods of authentication is provided in Appendix G.

Opportunity to Cross-Examine Witnesses and Inspect Exhibits

The opportunity for a party to cross-examine witnesses and inspect exhibits is a due-process protection that complements the right to offer evidence at a hearing. Cross-examination and inspection of exhibits build upon the foundation of reliability provided by the evidentiary guidelines set out above by subjecting competent testimony and authentic exhibits to adversarial testing. As with presentation of evidence, only persons with an interest in the proceeding sufficient to entitle them to participate in the hearing as a party should be permitted to engage in cross-examination and inspection of exhibits.

As noted above, appellate boards have significant discretion to control the manner in which parties are permitted to participate in a hearing. Some jurisdictions may choose to allow dog owners to pose cross-examination questions to witnesses directly. Others may choose to require that these questions be submitted to and posed by members of the board on the dog owner's behalf. Even if a jurisdiction otherwise chooses to conduct hearings with limited cross-examination, a dog owner should be permitted a reasonable opportunity to directly inspect any exhibits that are presented as support for a finding by the board that a dog is potentially dangerous.

Much of the testing of evidence presented to the board by an owner can be accomplished by board members, who may pose their own questions to witnesses and examine exhibits presented by the owner.

Rendering a Decision Supported by Competent, Substantial, and Material Evidence

An appellate board's ultimate responsibility at a hearing is to render a final decision of whether a dog is a potentially dangerous dog under state law. Due-process principles require that this decision be supported by competent, substantial, and material evidence that has been presented at the hearing. Adhering to the evidentiary guidelines discussed above will ensure that the record before the board consists of competent, substantial, and material evidence.[59]

It is likely at a hearing that there will be dispute over some of the facts of the incident at issue. In reaching a final decision, the board must weigh the evidence presented to resolve factual disputes to the best of its ability. Factors to be considered when weighing the evidence include the relative amount of evidence and the credibility of witnesses supporting one side of the dispute or the other. In weighing the evidence, the board acts as what is called in legal terminology the *finder of fact*.

After resolving disputed facts, the appellate board ultimately must determine whether there is competent, substantial, and material evidence to support a determination that the dog is potentially dangerous under state law. This process of making an ultimate determination is known in legal terminology as making a *conclusion of law*.

Findings of Fact and Conclusions of Law

An appellate board is responsible for resolving factual disputes by weighing the strength of the evidence that has been presented. After weighing the evidence, the appellate board must make a conclusion of law on whether a dog is a potentially dangerous dog.

An issue that affects how an appellate board makes a conclusion of law is the question of who bears the *burden of proof* at the hearing. In criminal trials, for example, the prosecution bears the burden of proving that the defendant is guilty. The allocation of the burden of proof is not clear-cut in dangerous-dog hearings, and a board has discretion to choose between one of the two approaches described below.

Usually in appellate proceedings, the appealing party bears the burden of proof and must present evidence and argument showing that the decision being appealed

---

59. Requiring that witnesses be sworn and have firsthand knowledge of the facts to which they testify helps ensure that evidence is competent. Requiring that evidence be relevant and probative helps ensure that it is material and substantial. *See generally* Quasi-Judicial Handbook, ch. 5 (discussing court opinions defining competent, material, and substantial evidence).

is wrong. Under this approach, a dog owner would bear the burden of showing that the initial determination was wrong.

In dangerous-dog proceedings, however, the hearing before the appellate board may be the first time that evidence is subjected to meaningful testing and the owner's side of the story is fully heard.[60] This makes the hearing quite different from typical legal appeals, which usually follow more formal adversarial proceedings. Accordingly, it may be appropriate for an appellate board to render its final decision based not on whether the owner has shown the initial determination to be wrong but on whether the evidence presented at the hearing satisfies the board that the dog is a potentially dangerous dog. Under this approach, the appellate board's decision resembles an initial dangerous-dog determination but comes after a more formal procedure.

Allocating the Burden of Proof

State law does not specify how the burden of proof is allocated in a dangerous-dog proceeding. An appellate board may either
- place the burden on the owner to prove that the initial decision was wrong or
- require evidence proving that the dog is potentially dangerous to be presented at the hearing.

In thinking about allocation of the burden of proof, it may be helpful to review the two sample forms for rendering a final decision provided in Appendix F. One sample illustrates an initial-determination-style allocation while the other illustrates an appeal-style allocation.

While an appellate board may allocate the burden of proof under either of the approaches discussed above, the burden should be allocated consistently in every dangerous-dog hearing. A board should not place the burden in some cases on the owner to show that the initial decision was wrong but in other cases allocate the burden in a manner resembling an initial determination.

An appellate board should have a clear standard for deciding whether the burden of proof, however allocated, has been met. In legal terminology, this is called the *standard of proof.* In a criminal case, for example, the prosecution must meet the standard of proof of showing a defendant's guilt beyond a reasonable doubt. State law does not define a standard of proof for dangerous-dog proceedings, and local governments have discretion to choose a standard appropriate for their community.

---

60. Recall that the initial decision of whether a dog is a potentially dangerous dog may be made summarily in many jurisdictions.

Table 1 lists common standards of proof that are used in legal proceedings. It also provides the approximate certainty that a decision-maker should have in order to meet the given standard of proof. For example, if an appellate board allocates the burden of proof similar to an initial determination and uses a preponderance-of-the-evidence standard of proof, each member will determine, based upon the record evidence, whether it is more likely than not that a dog is potentially dangerous under state law. As another example, if an appellate board allocates the burden of proof similar to a traditional appeal and uses a clear-and-convincing-evidence standard of proof, each member will determine whether they are reasonably confident that the owner has shown the initial dangerous-dog determination was wrong.

Table 1. Common Standards of Proof and the Approximate Certainty Required to Meet Them

Standard of proof	Approximate certainty
Beyond a reasonable doubt	Virtually certain (>99%)
Clear and convincing evidence	Reasonably confident (>75%)
Preponderance of the evidence	More likely than not (>50%)

While it is difficult to define standards of proof in concrete terms, for dangerous-dog proceedings it is sufficient to understand that a board should apply a specific standard and should articulate that standard when rendering a final decision.

As with the allocation of the burden of proof, the standard of proof used by an appellate board should be consistent in every hearing. A board should not, for example, require clear and convincing evidence in some cases and a preponderance of the evidence in others.

While somewhat technical, understanding the burden of proof and standard of proof ultimately helps to simplify the board's responsibility of rendering a final decision by clarifying which party must prove its case and what standard of evidence should guide the board's judgment.

After all evidence has been presented, the board members must deliberate to reach a final decision. Deliberation can be accomplished by board members discussing the case among themselves in open session and then voting on whether the standard of proof has been met. It may be desirable to make a statement before beginning deliberation that states the ultimate issue before the board, explains how the burden of proof is allocated, states the standard of proof, and provides an overview of the board's deliberative process.[61] A sample predeliberation statement is provided in Appendix E.

In rendering its final decision, the board may wish to make a statement reiterating the ultimate issue before the board; acknowledging that its decision is based on the competent, substantial, and material evidence in the record; stating its final decision based on the standard of proof; explaining the dog owner's right to appeal an adverse decision; and identifying the restrictions and other consequences of dangerous-dog ownership. While not explicitly required by state law, it is advisable that an appellate board render its final decision in writing.[62] Sample forms for rendering a final decision are provided in Appendix F.

Deliberating and Reaching a Final Decision

After all evidence is presented, the appellate board deliberates by discussing the case in open session and reaches a final decision by a vote of board members. It is advisable that the board's final decision be made in writing.

While the principle may be intuitive, it is worth explicitly noting that if an appellate board's final decision is that a dog is not potentially dangerous, no one can make a later decision to the contrary based on the same incident.[63] The initial decision-maker should not attempt to redeclare the dog to be potentially dangerous in contravention of the board's decision, and the board itself should not attempt to later revisit its own decision. However, the dog may be determined to be a potentially dangerous dog at a later time on the basis of a different incident.

De Novo Review in Superior Court

If an appellate board determines that a dog is a potentially dangerous dog, the owner may appeal the board's decision to the superior court of the county in which the appellate board is located.[64] To do so, the owner must file a notice of appeal and a petition for review in the superior court.[65]

The proceeding in superior court is *de novo*, meaning that it is an entirely new hearing that is conducted as if no hearing had been held by the appellate board.[66]

---

61. *See generally* Quasi-Judicial Handbook, ch. 5 (suggesting such a statement for land use boards).

62. Issuing a written decision with findings of fact is a common due-process requirement. *See, e.g.,* Wolff v. McDonnell, 418 U.S. 539, 563 (1974).

63. *Cf. In re* Mitchell, 88 N.C. App. 602, 605 (1988) (explaining that this legal principle, known as *res judicata*, applies to quasi-judicial decisions).

64. G.S. 67-4.1(c).

65. *Id.*

66. Caswell County v. Hanks, 120 N.C. App. 489, 491 (1995).

The superior court judge must hear the case on the merits "from beginning to end . . . and without any presumption in favor of the [appellate board's] decision."[67] Evidence should be presented anew, and the judge should make independent findings of fact that support a conclusion of law on whether the dog is a potentially dangerous dog under state law.[68] An owner may wish to be represented in superior court by an attorney, and the local government is likely to be represented by the municipal or county attorney.

Unlike appellate-board hearings, the rules of evidence and the rules of civil procedure apply to superior court hearings.[69] Otherwise, the general approach outlined in this publication with respect to appellate-board hearings may be a useful reference for superior court proceedings. A dog owner has the right to appeal an adverse decision in superior court to the North Carolina Court of Appeals.[70]

---

67. *Id.*

68. *Id.* (trial court erred by relying solely on record evidence from the appellate-board hearing and failing to make independent findings of fact).

69. *See* North Carolina Rules of Evidence, G.S. 8C-1, r. 1101(a); North Carolina Rules of Civil Procedure, G.S. 1A-1, r. 52. The applicability of the rules of evidence may have little practical consequence as trial judges are presumed to disregard incompetent evidence when acting as finders of fact. *Cf.* State v. Cheeks, 267 N.C. App. 579 (2019) (so explaining in the context of criminal bench trials), *aff'd*, 377 N.C. 528 (2021). A notable consequence of the applicability of the rules of civil procedure is that the presiding superior court judge should be careful to make specific findings of the ultimate facts of the case and a separate statement of the conclusions of law. *See, e.g.,* Farmers Bank v. Michael T. Brown Distribs., Inc., 307 N.C. 342, 347 (1983) (describing this requirement under the rules of civil procedure and noting that well-articulated findings and conclusions facilitate appellate review).

70. *See* G.S. 7A-27(b)(1); *Hanks,* 120 N.C. App. at 490 (considering such an appeal).

Appendixes

Appendix A. Initial Dangerous-Dog Determination

The following form is a sample that may be used to make an initial dangerous-dog determination and notify a dog owner of the determination.

DANGEROUS-DOG DETERMINATION
Investigator's name:
Date of incident:
Location of incident:
Dog owner: *Provide owner's name, address, phone number, or other contact information*
Dog: *Identify dog, including name and physical description*
Factual Basis
Investigation report: *Provide a detailed narrative of the facts discovered during the investigation of the incident, attaching additional pages if necessary. Conclude the narrative with the following sentence: "The investigation has not revealed facts suggesting that any exception listed in G.S. 67-4.1(b) applies to this incident."*
Documentary evidence (yes/no):   *If yes, briefly describe and attach any photos, videos, medical records, etc.*
Determination that Dog Is a Potentially Dangerous Dog
Based on the factual basis set out above, the dog hereby is determined to be a potentially dangerous dog under Article 1A of Chapter 67 of the North Carolina General Statutes because there is a reasonably reliable basis to believe that the dog (check one or more below)
Inflicted a bite on a person resulting in broken bones or disfiguring lacerations or requiring cosmetic surgery or hospitalization
Killed or inflicted severe injury upon a domestic animal while not on the owner's real property
Approached a person in a vicious or terrorizing manner in an apparent attitude of attack while not on the owner's property
Notice to Owner
Your dog is determined to be a potentially dangerous dog under Article 1A of Chapter 67 of the North Carolina General Statutes. It is unlawful for you to leave the dog unattended on your property unless the dog is confined indoors, in a securely enclosed and locked pen, or in another structure designed to restrain the dog. It is unlawful for you to permit the dog to go beyond your property unless the dog is leashed and muzzled or is otherwise securely restrained and muzzled. If you transfer ownership or possession of the dog, you must provide written notice to the authority who made the determination that your dog is potentially dangerous, stating the name and address of the new owner or possessor of the dog. You also must provide written notice to the person taking ownership or possession of the dog, specifying the dog's dangerous behavior and the authority's determination that the dog is a potentially dangerous dog.   You may appeal this determination by filing a written objection within three days of receiving the determination with [*identify appellate board*].   *Optionally, attach form for making objection.*
Date: Investigator's signature:

Appendix B. Objection to Initial Dangerous-Dog Determination

The following form is a sample that may be used by a dog owner to object to an initial dangerous-dog determination and receive a hearing before a local appellate board.

OBJECTION TO DANGEROUS-DOG DETERMINATION
Dog owner:
Provide name, address, phone number, or other contact information
Dog:
Identify dog
Investigator name:
Date of determination:
Appellate board:
Identify appellate board to which objection is directed
Basis of Objection
The undersigned dog owner objects to the attached dangerous-dog determination as follows:
Provide an explanation of your objection to the determination that the dog is a potentially dangerous dog and the determination's factual basis. Attach a copy of the determination.
Documentary evidence (yes/no):
Circle yes if you want to present documentary evidence (photos, documents, witness statements, etc.) at the hearing. Briefly describe that evidence.
Witness testimony or statements (yes/no):
Circle yes if you wish to provide witness testimony or statements at the hearing. Identify witnesses and briefly describe their testimony or statement.
Date: Dog owner's signature:

Appendix C. Notice of Appellate-Board Hearing

The following form is a sample that may be used to notify a dog owner of the scheduling of an appellate-board hearing following the owner's filing of written objections to an initial determination. This sample presumes that the appellate board uses an initial-determination-style burden of proof and a preponderance-of-the-evidence standard of proof, issues discussed in more detail in the main text.

NOTICE OF DANGEROUS-DOG HEARING	
Dog owner:	
Provide name, address, phone number, or other contact information	
Dog:	
Identify dog	
Investigator's name:	
Date of initial determination:	Date objection filed:
Hearing Scheduled	
Having received the attached objection to the attached dangerous-dog determination [*attach copy of objection and initial determination*], a hearing before the [*identify appellate board*] is scheduled as follows:	
Hearing date:	
Hearing time:	
Hearing location:	
Nature of Hearing	
Under the law, [*dog owner*] is entitled to an opportunity to be heard before [*identify appellate board*] on the objection to the determination that [*identify dog*] is a potentially dangerous dog under Article 1A of Chapter 67 of the North Carolina General Statutes.	
[*Dog owner*] may make a presentation to the board as follows:	
Briefly describe local practice concerning the manner in which a dog owner may present argument, testimony from witnesses, and other evidence to the appellate board.	
Standard for Board's Decision	
The board's duty is to weigh the evidence to determine whether the board is satisfied by a preponderance of the evidence that [*identify dog*] is a potentially dangerous dog.	
Right to Appeal	
[*Dog owner*] has the right to appeal the board's decision to superior court by filing a notice of appeal and petition for review within ten days of the board's final decision.	
Date:	Signature of board chair or designee:

Appendix D. The Opening Statement at an Appellate-Board Hearing

Sample Chart of Opening-Statement Components

The following chart illustrates the components that an appellate board may wish to integrate into an opening statement for dangerous-dog hearings. Note that the chart illustrates two alternative burdens of proof for the board's decision, each using a preponderance-of-the-evidence standard of proof, issues discussed in more detail in the main text. The component parts may be modified to conform to local practice.

INITIAL DETERMINATION AND BASIS FOR APPEAL		
[Dog owner] has filed a written objection to the determination on [date of initial determination] by [person or board making initial determination] that [identify dog] is a potentially dangerous dog under Article 1A of Chapter 67 of the North Carolina General Statutes. [Identify dog] was determined to be a potentially dangerous dog on the following basis: Set out basis for initial determination; enter associated written documentation into the record		
Roles of Participants and Disclosures		
Under the law, [dog owner] is entitled to a hearing before this board. This hearing is open for the public to observe, but participation is limited to [dog owner], board members, and [identify any other person, if any, with a special interest in the hearing sufficient to permit participation]. At this time, all board members are asked to disclose any conflict of interest, bias, or ex parte communication concerning this matter.		
Hearing Procedure		
During this hearing, board members may make statements, call and question witnesses, and present exhibits. [Dog owner] also may make statements, call witnesses, and present exhibits to the board. [Dog owner] will have an opportunity to present questions to any adverse witnesses and examine any adverse evidence.		
Evidentiary Guidelines		
The evidence presented at this hearing must be relevant, probative, and authentic. Witnesses should focus their testimony on facts and not personal opinion. The board may exercise its discretion to exclude evidence that does not meet these guidelines.		
Standard for Board's Decision		
Appeal style	The board's duty is to weigh the evidence to determine whether [dog owner] has shown by a preponderance of the evidence that the initial determination that [identify dog] is a potentially dangerous dog was wrong.	
Initial-determination style	The board's duty is to weigh the evidence to determine whether the board is satisfied by a preponderance of the evidence that [identify dog] is a potentially dangerous dog.	
Right to Appeal		
[Dog owner] has the right to appeal the board's decision by filing a notice of appeal and petition for review in superior court within ten days of the board's final decision.		
Administration of Oath		
Witnesses must swear or affirm their testimony. At this time, we will administer the oath to all witnesses.		

Sample Opening Statement

This opening statement uses the components of the chart above with a fictitious example to illustrate how an opening statement may be delivered at a hearing. This sample uses an initial-determination-style burden of proof and a preponderance-of-the-evidence standard of proof.

Doris Douglas has filed a written objection to the determination on June 9, 2024, by Animal Services Officer Sam Smith that Ms. Douglas's dog Spike, a white and black terrier mix, is a potentially dangerous dog under Article 1A of Chapter 67 of the North Carolina General Statutes. Smith determined that Spike was a potentially dangerous dog on the following basis:

On June 8, 2024, Officer Sam Smith received a call from Cathy Cobb reporting that her dog Lulu, a brown dachshund, was attacked by a white and black terrier at the municipal dog park on Main Street. Smith responded to Healthy Paws animal hospital, where Cobb had taken Lulu for treatment. During his investigation, Smith learned that Lulu suffered a broken leg and that the dog that attacked Lulu was owned by Doris Douglas and named Spike.

Additional details, including photographs and veterinary records, are set out in Officer Smith's dangerous-dog determination, which we now introduce into the record as Exhibit 1.

Under the law, Ms. Douglas is entitled to a hearing before this board. This hearing is open for the public to observe, but participation is limited to Ms. Douglas and board members. At this time, all board members are asked to disclose any conflict of interest, bias, or ex parte communication concerning this matter. Hearing none, we will proceed.

During this hearing, board members may make statements, call and question witnesses, and present exhibits. Ms. Douglas also may make statements, call witnesses, and present exhibits to the board. Ms. Douglas will have an opportunity to present questions to any adverse witnesses and examine any adverse evidence.

The evidence presented at this hearing must be relevant, probative, and authentic. Witnesses should focus their testimony on facts and not personal opinion. The board may exercise its discretion to exclude evidence that does not meet these guidelines.

The board's duty is to weigh the evidence to determine whether the board is satisfied by a preponderance of the evidence that Ms. Douglas's dog Spike is a potentially dangerous dog.

Ms. Douglas has the right to appeal the board's decision to superior court by filing a notice of appeal and petition for review in superior court within ten days of the board's final decision.

Witnesses must swear or affirm their testimony. At this time, we will administer the oath to all witnesses.

Appendix E. Predeliberation Statement

Sample Chart of Predeliberation-Statement Components

The following chart illustrates the components that an appellate board may wish to integrate into a predeliberation statement for dangerous-dog hearings. Note that the chart illustrates two alternative burdens of proof for the board's decision, each using a preponderance-of-the-evidence standard of proof, issues discussed in more detail in the main text. An appellate board may modify the component parts as appropriate for local practice.

DELIBERATION PROCEDURE	
Having heard the evidence, board members now will deliberate and vote to reach a final decision in this case. This proceeding remains open for the public to observe, but only board members may participate in deliberation. When our deliberation has concluded, the board will announce its final decision and render the decision in writing.	
Evidence to Be Considered	
During deliberation, the board will consider the competent, material, and substantial evidence that has been presented at this hearing.	
Standard for Board's Decision	
Appeal style	The board's duty is to weigh the evidence to determine whether [*dog owner*] has shown by a preponderance of the evidence that the initial determination that [*identify dog*] is a potentially dangerous dog was wrong.
Initial-determination style	The board's duty is to weigh the evidence to determine whether the board is satisfied by a preponderance of the evidence that [*identify dog*] is a potentially dangerous dog.
Voting	
Each board member will vote based on whether they individually are satisfied that this standard has been met. The board's final decision will be based on majority vote.	
Right to Appeal	
[*Dog owner*] has the right to appeal the board's decision to superior court by filing a notice of appeal and petition for review within ten days of the board's final decision.	
Opening of Deliberations	
We will now begin deliberation. [*Identify board member*], you are recognized to state your view of this case. [*Continue recognizing each board member in turn or otherwise deliberating.*]	

Sample Predeliberation Statement

This statement uses the components of the chart above with a fictitious example to illustrate how a predeliberation statement may be delivered at a hearing. It uses an initial-determination-style burden of proof and a preponderance-of-the-evidence standard of proof.

Having heard the evidence, board members now will deliberate and vote to reach a final decision in this case. This proceeding remains open for the public to observe, but only board members may participate in deliberation. When our deliberation has concluded, the board will announce its final decision and render the decision in writing.

During deliberation, the board will consider the competent, material, and substantial evidence that has been presented at this hearing.

The board's duty is to weigh the evidence to determine whether the board is satisfied by a preponderance of the evidence that Doris Douglas's dog Spike is a potentially dangerous dog.

Each board member will vote based on whether they individually are satisfied that this standard has been met. The board's final decision will be based on majority vote.

Ms. Douglas has the right to appeal the board's decision to superior court by filing a notice of appeal and petition for review within ten days of the board's final decision.

We will now begin deliberation. Mr. Allen, you are recognized to state your view of this case.

Appendix F. Appellate-Board Final Decision

This sample form uses an initial-determination-style burden of proof and a preponderance-of-the-evidence standard of proof, issues discussed in more detail in the main text. The form may be modified to conform to local practice.

DANGEROUS-DOG DETERMINATION	
Board:	
Date of hearing:	
Dog owner:	
Provide owner's name, address, phone number or other contact information	
Dog:	
Identify dog, including name and physical description	
Findings of Fact	
State the details of the initial determination to which the dog owner objected. Describe the evidence presented at the hearing, attaching additional pages if necessary. If there is a dispute over an important fact at the hearing, state how the board resolved that dispute.	
Attach a copy of the initial determination to which the dog owner objected. Attach copies of any exhibits that were presented at the hearing to the extent feasible. Conclude the narrative with the following sentence: "The board does not find that any exception listed in G.S. 67-4.1(b) applies to this incident."	
Final Determination that Dog Is a Potentially Dangerous Dog	
Based on the findings of fact set out above, the dog hereby is determined to be a potentially dangerous dog under Article 1A of Chapter 67 of the North Carolina General Statutes because a preponderance of the evidence shows that the dog (check one or more below)	
	Inflicted a bite on a person resulting in broken bones or disfiguring lacerations or requiring cosmetic surgery or hospitalization
	Killed or inflicted severe injury upon a domestic animal while not on the owner's real property
	Approached a person in a vicious or terrorizing manner in an apparent attitude of attack while not on the owner's property
Notice to Owner	
Your dog is determined to be a potentially dangerous dog under Article 1A of Chapter 67 of the North Carolina General Statutes. It is unlawful for you to leave the dog unattended on your property unless the dog is confined indoors, in a securely enclosed and locked pen, or in another structure designed to restrain the dog. It is unlawful for you to permit the dog to go beyond your property unless the dog is leashed and muzzled or is otherwise securely restrained and muzzled. If you transfer ownership or possession of the dog, you must provide written notice to the authority who made the determination that your dog is potentially dangerous, stating the name and address of the new owner or possessor of the dog. You also must provide written notice to the person taking ownership or possession of the dog, specifying the dog's dangerous behavior and the authority's determination that the dog is a potentially dangerous dog.	
Right to Appeal	
You may appeal this determination by filing a notice of appeal and petition for review in superior court within ten days of the board's final decision.	
Date of decision:	Signature of board chair or designee:

This sample form uses an appeal-style burden of proof and a preponderance-of-the-evidence standard of proof, issues discussed in more detail in the main text. The form may be modified to conform to local practice.

DANGEROUS-DOG DETERMINATION
Board:
Date of hearing:
Dog owner:
Provide owner's name, address, phone number, or other contact information
Dog:
Identify dog, including name and physical description
Findings of Fact
State the details of the initial determination to which the dog owner objected. Describe the evidence presented at the hearing, attaching additional pages if necessary. If there is a dispute over an important fact at the hearing, state how the board resolved that dispute.   *Attach a copy of the initial determination to which the dog owner objected. Attach copies of any exhibits that were presented at the hearing to the extent feasible. Conclude the narrative with the following sentence: "The board does not find that any exception listed in G.S. 67-4.1(b) applies to this incident."*
Final Determination that Dog Is a Potentially Dangerous Dog
Based on the findings of fact set out above, the dog hereby is determined to be a potentially dangerous dog under Article 1A of Chapter 67 of the North Carolina General Statutes because the dog owner has not shown by a preponderance of the evidence that the initial determination to which the owner objected was erroneous.
Notice to Owner
Your dog is determined to be a potentially dangerous dog under Article 1A of Chapter 67 of the North Carolina General Statutes. It is unlawful for you to leave the dog unattended on your property unless the dog is confined indoors, in a securely enclosed and locked pen, or in another structure designed to restrain the dog. It is unlawful for you to permit the dog to go beyond your property unless the dog is leashed and muzzled or is otherwise securely restrained and muzzled. If you transfer ownership or possession of the dog, you must provide written notice to the authority who made the determination that your dog is potentially dangerous, stating the name and address of the new owner or possessor of the dog. You also must provide written notice to the person taking ownership or possession of the dog, specifying the dog's dangerous behavior and the authority's determination that the dog is a potentially dangerous dog.
Right to Appeal
You may appeal this determination by filing a notice of appeal and petition for review in superior court within ten days of the board's final decision.
Date of decision:	Signature of board chair or designee:

Appendix G. Common Nontestimonial Evidence and Methods of Authentication

The following are common forms of nontestimonial evidence that may be offered at a dangerous-dog hearing, each with a nonexhaustive list of methods by which this evidence may be authenticated.

Medical records
- Health-care provider's testimony or statement
- Treated patient's testimony or statement
- Official or distinctive markings on the face of the record
- Explanation of the chain of custody

Photographs or video
- Photographer's testimony or statement
- Electronic metadata
- Explanation of the chain of custody

Reports from police or animal services
- Testimony or statement of the investigator or the custodian of records
- Official or distinctive markings on the face of the record
- Explanation of the chain of custody

Veterinary records
- Testimony or statement of a veterinary-care provider
- Testimony or statement of the owner of a treated animal
- Official or distinctive markings on the face of the record
- Explanation of the chain of custody

Property boundaries or maps
- Testimony or statement of a witness familiar with the depicted property
- Official or distinctive markings on the face of the record

Electronic communications
- Communication participants' testimonies or statements
- Electronic metadata
- Explanation of the chain of custody

Appendix H. Text of North Carolina General Statute Chapter 67, Article 1A

§ 67-4.1. Definitions and procedures.

(a) As used in this Article, unless the context clearly requires otherwise and except as modified in subsection (b) of this section, the term:

    (1)   "Dangerous dog" means

        a.   A dog that:

            1.   Without provocation has killed or inflicted severe injury on a person; or

            2.   Is determined by the person or Board designated by the county or municipal authority responsible for animal control to be potentially dangerous because the dog has engaged in one or more of the behaviors listed in subdivision (2) of this subsection.

        b.   Any dog owned or harbored primarily or in part for the purpose of dog fighting, or any dog trained for dog fighting.

    (2)   "Potentially dangerous dog" means a dog that the person or Board designated by the county or municipal authority responsible for animal control determines to have:

        a.   Inflicted a bite on a person that resulted in broken bones or disfiguring lacerations or required cosmetic surgery or hospitalization; or

        b.   Killed or inflicted severe injury upon a domestic animal when not on the owner's real property; or

        c.   Approached a person when not on the owner's property in a vicious or terrorizing manner in an apparent attitude of attack.

    (3)   "Owner" means any person or legal entity that has a possessory property right in a dog.

    (4)   "Owner's real property" means any real property owned or leased by the owner of the dog, but does not include any public right-of-way or a common area of a condominium, apartment complex, or townhouse development.

    (5)   "Severe injury" means any physical injury that results in broken bones or disfiguring lacerations or required cosmetic surgery or hospitalization.

(b) The provisions of this Article do not apply to:

    (1)   A dog being used by a law enforcement officer to carry out the law enforcement officer's official duties;

    (2)   A dog being used in a lawful hunt;

    (3)   A dog where the injury or damage inflicted by the dog was sustained by a domestic animal while the dog was working as a hunting dog, herding dog, or predator control dog on the property of, or under the control of, its owner or keeper, and the damage or injury was to a species or type of domestic animal appropriate to the work of the dog; or

    (4)   A dog where the injury inflicted by the dog was sustained by a person who, at the time of the injury, was committing a willful trespass or other tort, was tormenting, abusing, or assaulting the dog, had tormented, abused, or assaulted the dog, or was committing or attempting to commit a crime.

(c) The county or municipal authority responsible for animal control shall designate a person or a Board to be responsible for determining when a dog is a "potentially dangerous dog" and shall designate a separate Board to hear any appeal. The person or Board making the determination that a dog is a "potentially dangerous dog" must notify the owner in writing, giving the reasons for the determination, before the dog may be considered potentially dangerous under this Article. The owner may appeal the determination by filing written objections with the appellate Board within three days. The appellate Board shall schedule a hearing within 10 days of the filing of the objections. Any appeal from the final decision of such appellate Board shall be taken to the superior court by filing notice of appeal and a petition for review within 10 days of the final decision of the appellate Board. Appeals from rulings of the appellate Board shall be heard in the superior court division. The appeal shall be heard de novo before a superior court judge sitting in the county in which the appellate Board whose ruling is being appealed is located. (1989 (Reg. Sess., 1990), c. 1023, s. 1.)

§ 67-4.2. Precautions against attacks by dangerous dogs.

(a) It is unlawful for an owner to:
- (1)   Leave a dangerous dog unattended on the owner's real property unless the dog is confined indoors, in a securely enclosed and locked pen, or in another structure designed to restrain the dog;
- (2)   Permit a dangerous dog to go beyond the owner's real property unless the dog is leashed and muzzled or is otherwise securely restrained and muzzled.

(b) If the owner of a dangerous dog transfers ownership or possession of the dog to another person (as defined in G.S. 12-3(6)), the owner shall provide written notice to:
- (1)   The authority that made the determination under this Article, stating the name and address of the new owner or possessor of the dog; and
- (2)   The person taking ownership or possession of the dog, specifying the dog's dangerous behavior and the authority's determination.

(c) Violation of this section is a Class 3 misdemeanor. (1989 (Reg. Sess., 1990), c. 1023; 1993, c. 539, s. 532; 1994, Ex. Sess., c. 24, s. 14(c).)

§ 67-4.3. Penalty for attacks by dangerous dogs.

The owner of a dangerous dog that attacks a person and causes physical injuries requiring medical treatment in excess of one hundred dollars ($100.00) shall be guilty of a Class 1 misdemeanor. (1989 (Reg. Sess., 1990), c. 1023; 1993, c. 539, s. 533; 1994, Ex. Sess., c. 24, s. 14(c).)

§ 67-4.4. Strict liability.

The owner of a dangerous dog shall be strictly liable in civil damages for any injuries or property damage the dog inflicts upon a person, his property, or another animal. (1989 (Reg. Sess., 1990), c. 1023, s. 1.)

§ 67-4.5. Local ordinances.

Nothing in this Article shall be construed to prevent a city or county from adopting or enforcing its own program for control of dangerous dogs. (1989 (Reg. Sess., 1990), c. 1023, s. 1.)